# Music of The Stars

## SONGS RECORDED by NANCY WILSON

Produced by **JOHN L. HAAG**

Sales and Shipping:

**PROFESSIONAL MUSIC INSTITUTE** LLC
1336 Cruzero Street, Box 128, Ojai, CA 93024
info@promusicbooks.com   www.promusicbooks.com

T0050710

# Don't Go To Strangers

Lyric by Redd Evans
Music by Arthur Kent and Dave Mann

4

# As Long As He Needs Me

*(from the Columbia Pictures - Romulus Film "Oliver!")*

Lyric and Music by
Lionel Bart

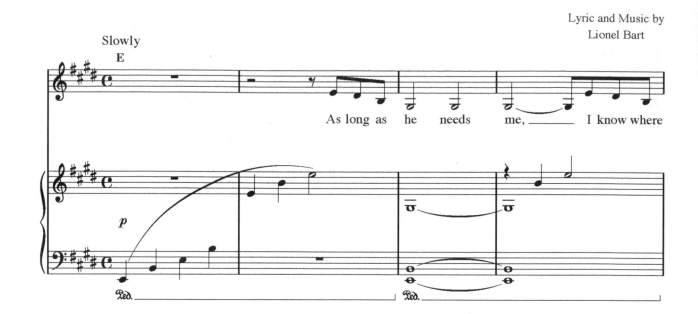

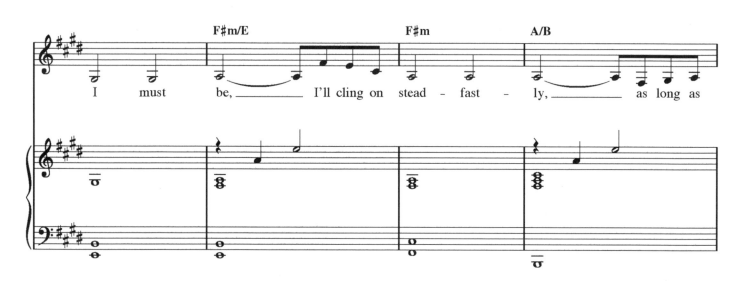

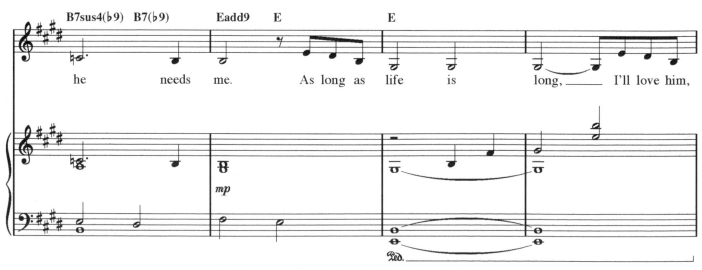

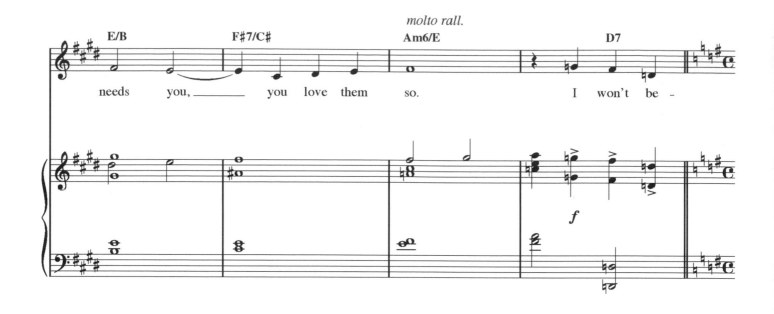

needs you, _____ you love them so. I won't be -

- tray his trust, _____ though peo-ple say I must, _____ I've got to

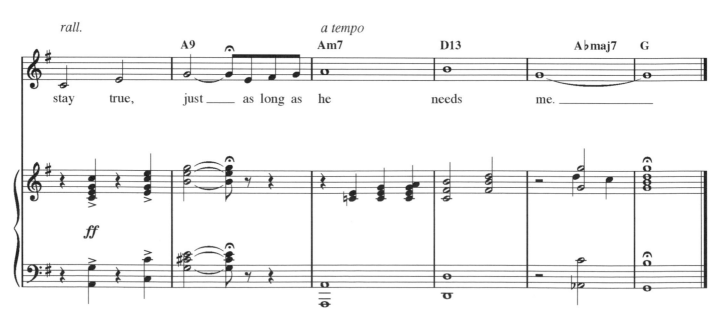

stay true, just _____ as long as he needs me. _____

As long as he needs me 5-5

# Back In Your Own Backyard

Lyric and Music by
Al Jolson, Billy Rose and Dave Dreyer

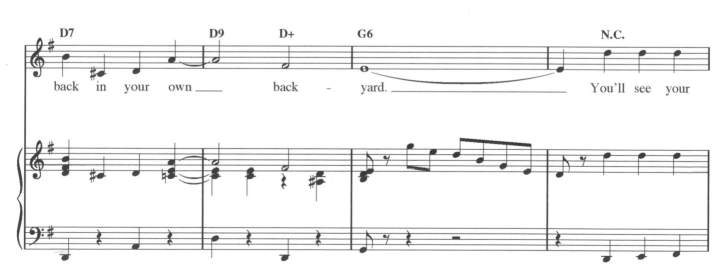

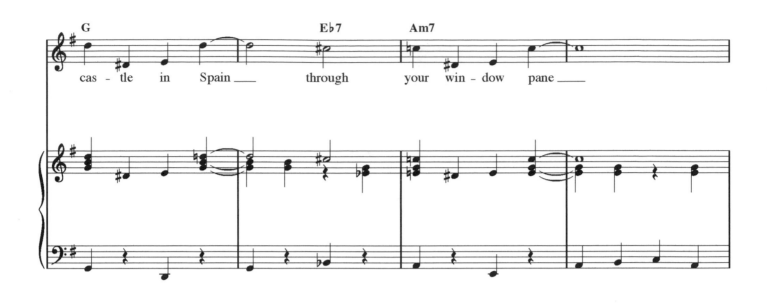

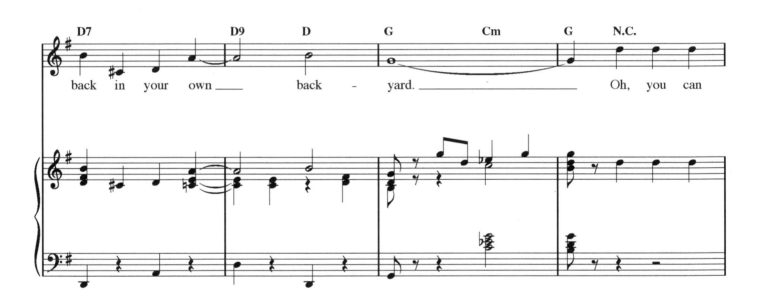

# But Beautiful

Lyric by Johnny Burke
Music by Jimmy Van Heusen

# Close Your Eyes

Lyric and Music by
Bernice Petkere

18

# Don't Take Your Love From Me

Lyric and Music by
Henry Nemo

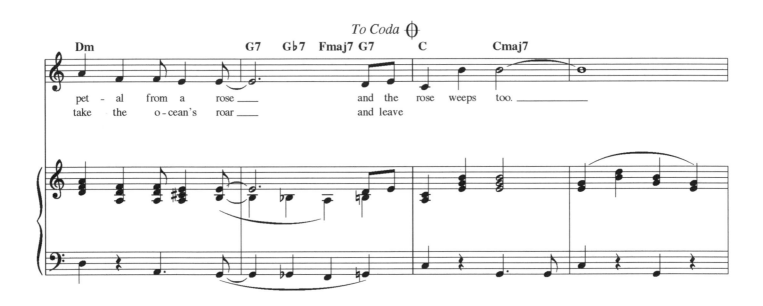

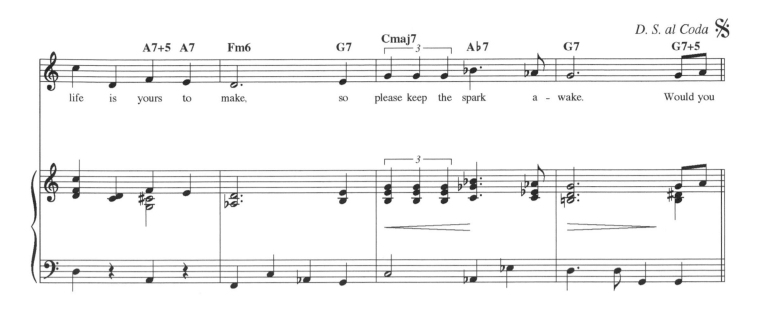

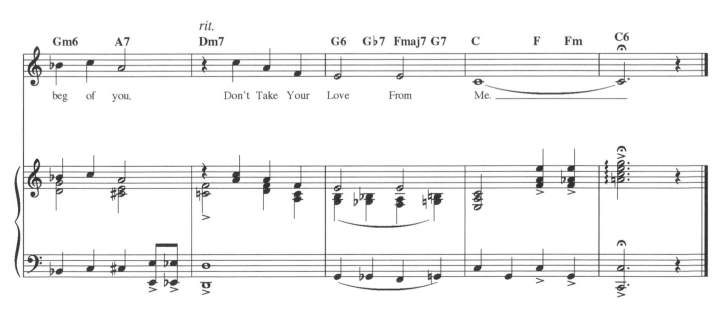

Don't take your love from me 2-2

# Fly Me To The Moon

Lyric and Music by
Bart Howard

26

Fly me to the moon 5-7

Fly ____ me to the moon, and let me play ____ among the stars, let __ me see what spring is like ____ on __ Ju – pi – ter __ and Mars. __ In oth – er words, ___

# I'm Always Drunk In San Francisco

Lyric and Music by
Tommy Wolf

I'm always drunk in San Francisco 3-3

# Free Again
## (Non... C'est Rien)

English Lyric and Musical Adaptation by Robert Colby
French Lyric by Michael Jourdan
Music by Armand Canfora and Joss Baselli

# Non... C'est Rien

## (Free Again)

English Lyric and Musical Adaptation by Robert Colby
French Lyric by Michael Jourdan
Music by Armand Canfora and Joss Baselli

Non, c'est rien
Ou si peu croyez-le bien,
Ça ira mieux dès demain
Avec le temps qui passe
Dans la vie, tout s'efface
Non, c'est rien
A quoi bon tendre vos mains?
Je n'ai pas tant de chagrin
C'est vous qui êtes tristes
Mes amis, partez vite.

Laissez-moi
Cette nuit sortez
Mais sans moi
Allez boire à ma santé
Remportez vetre pitié
Vous me faites rire
Bien rire.

Non, c'est rien
Ou si peu croyez-le bien
Cet amour n'était plus rien
D'autre qu'une habitude
J'en ai la certitude
Non, c'est rien
Ce garçon moi, je le plains
Ne croyez pas que demain
Une seule seconde
Je serai seule au monde.

Laissez-moi
Cette nuit sortez
Mais sans moi
Allez boire à mes amous
A tous mes futurs amours
Mes prochains "Je t'aime"
"Je t'aime".

Laissez-moi
Et ne croyez pas,
Surtout pas,
Que je vais pleurer pour ça,
Seul mon coeur n'y comprends rien.
Mais à part ça rien,
Rien!

Non, c'est rien
Ou si peu croyez-le bien
Je n'ai pas tant de chagrin
Je n'ai pas tant de chagrin
Non, c'est rien
Non, c'est rien
Rien.

(Him)　　　　　　　　　(Him)
# I'll Only Miss Her When I Think Of Her
### (From The Broadway Musical "SKYSCRAPER")

Lyric by Sammy Cahn
Music by James Van Heusen

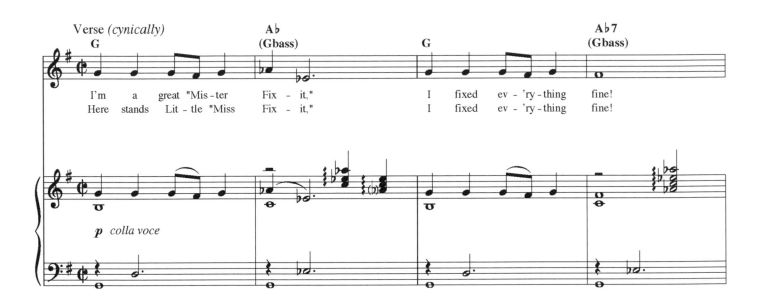

I'm a great "Mis-ter Fix-it," I fixed ev-'ry-thing fine!
Here stands Lit-tle "Miss Fix-it," I fixed ev-'ry-thing fine!

I fixed Geor-gi-na's fu-ture In hopes that I fixed mine!
I fixed ev-'ry-one's fu-ture But not like I fixed mine!

I'll only miss her when I think of her 2-4

I'll only miss her when I think of her 3-4

I'll only miss her when I think of her 4-4

# Gee Baby, Ain't I Good To You

Lyric by Don Redman and Andy Razaf
Music by Don Redman

*To Coda* ⊕

# Like Someone In Love

Lyric by Johnny Burke
Music by Jimmy Van Heusen

Chorus: *Slowly, with expression*

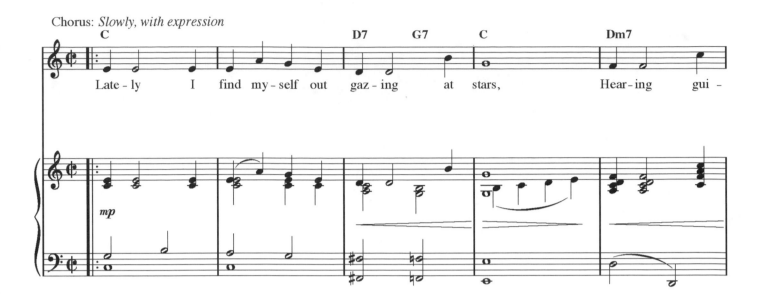

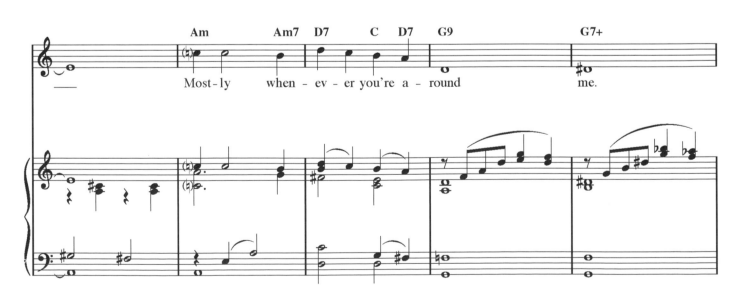

Like someone in love 3-3

# Here's That Rainy Day

Lyric and Music by
Johnny Burke and James Van Heusen

Slowly, with expression

Broadly *(with much feeling)*

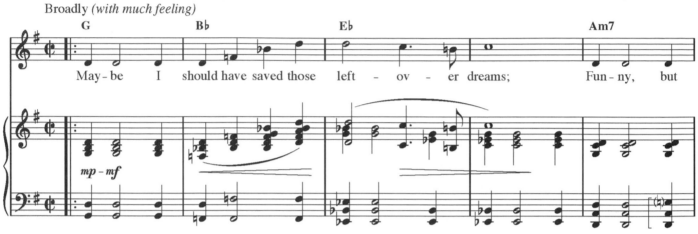

May-be I should have saved those left-ov-er dreams; Fun-ny, but

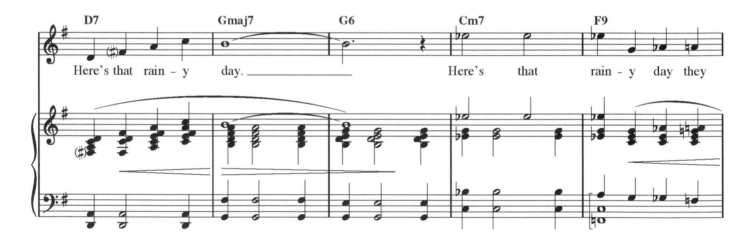

Here's that rain-y day. _____ Here's that rain-y day they

told me a-bout, And I laughed at the thought that it might turn out this

Here's that rainy day 2-2

# My Ship

*(from The Broadway Musical "Lady In The Dark")*

Lyric by Ira Gershwin
Music by Kurt Weill

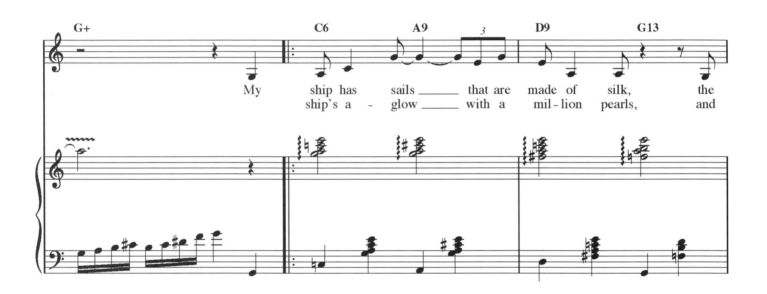

My ship has sails _____ that are made of silk, the
ship's a - glow _____ with a mil - lion pearls, and

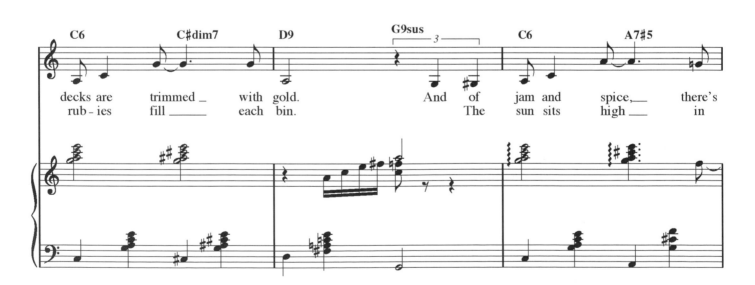

decks are trimmed _ with gold. And of jam and spice, _ there's
rub - ies fill _____ each bin. The sun sits high _____ in

# Our Day Will Come

Lyric by Bob Hilliard
Music by Mort Garson

Slowly, with expression

Our day will come and we'll have ev - 'ry-thing.

We'll share the joy fall - ing in love can bring. No one can

tell me that I'm too young to know, I love you so and you love

# Save Your Love For Me

Lyric and Music by
Buddy Johnson

# Unchain My Heart

Lyric and Music by
Bobby Sharp and Teddy Powell

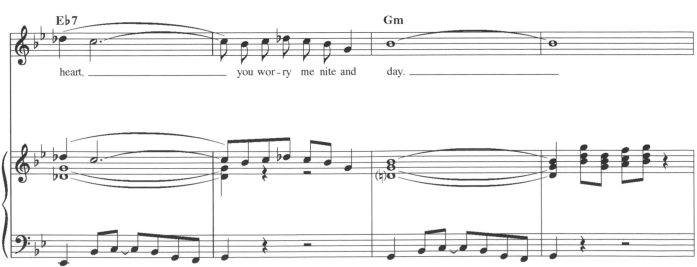

Unchain my heart 4-4

# When The World Was Young

## (Ah, The Apple Trees)

English Lyric by Johnny Mercer
French Lyric by Angele Vannier
Music by Philippe-Gerard

## FEMALE LYRICS

### VERSE 1.

They call me coquette, and mademoiselle,
And I must admit I like it quite well,
It's something to be the darling of all;
La grande femme fatale - the belle of the ball,
There's nothing as gay as life in Paris,
There's no other person, I'd rather be,
I love what I do - I love what I see,
But where is the school girl that used to be me...

### VERSE 2.

While sitting around we often recall,
The laugh of the year - the night of them all,
The blonde who was so attractive that year,
Some opening night that made us all cheer;
Remember that time we all got so tight,
And Jacques and Antoine got into a fight,
The gendarmes who came, passed out like a light,
I laugh with the rest - it's all very bright.

### VERSE 3.

You'll see me at Cape d'Antibes, or in Spain,
I follow the sun by boat or by plane,
It's any old millionaire in a storm,
For I've got my mink to keep my heart warm:
And, sometimes I drink too much with the crowd,
And, sometimes I talk a little too loud,
My head may be aching, but it's unbowed,
And sometimes I see it all through a cloud...

### CHORUS 1.

Ah, the apple trees,
Where at garden teas,
Jack-o-lanterns swung:
Fashions of the day,
Vests of applique,
Dresses of shantung,
Only yesterday,
When the world was young.

### CHORUS 2.

Ah, the apple trees,
Sunlit memories,
Where the hammock swung,
On our backs we'd lie;
Looking at the sky,
Till the stars were strung,
Only last July,
When the world was young.

### CHORUS 3.

Ah, the apple trees,
And the hive of bees,
Where we once got stung,
Summers at Bordeaux:
Rowing the bateau,
Where the willow hung,
Just a dream ago,
When the world was young.

## FRENCH LYRICS

### VERSE 1.

Le grand chevalier du coeur de Paris
Se rappelait plus du goût des prairies
Il faisait la guerre avec ses amis
Dedans la fumée dedans les metros
Desus les pavés dedans les victros
Il ne savait pas qu'il en etait saoul
Il ne savait pas qu'il dormait debout
Paris le tenait par la peau du cou

### VERSE 2.

Sous un pommier doux il l'a retrouvées
Croisant le soleil avec la rosée
Vivent les chansons pour les bienaimées
Je me souviens d'elle au sang de velours
Elle avait des mains qui parlaient d'amour
Et tressaient l'argile avec les nuages
Et pressaient le vent contre son visage
Pour en exprimer l'huile des voyages

### VERSE 3.

Adieu mon Paris, dit le chevalier
J'ai dormi cent ans debout sans manger
Les pommes d'argent de mes doux pommiers
Alors le village a crié si fort
Que toutes les fill's ont couru dehors
Mais le chevalier n'a salué qu'elle
Au sang de velours au coeur tant fidèle
Chevalier fera la guerre en dentelles

### REFRAIN:

Ah! les pommiers doux
Ronde et ritournelle
J'ai pas peur des loups
Chantonnait la belle
Ils sont pas mechants
Avec les enfants
Qu'ont le coeur fidèle
Et les genoux blancs.

### REFRAIN:

Ah! les pommiers doux
Ronde et ritournelle
J'ai pas peur des loups
Chantonnait la belle
Ils sont pas mechants
Avec les enfants
Qu'ont le coeur fidèle
Et les genoux blancs.

### REFRAIN:

Ah! les pommiers doux
Ronde et ritournelle
J'ai pas peur des loups
Chantonnait la belle
Ils sont pas mechants
Avec les enfants
Qu'ont le coeur fidèle
Et les genoux blancs.

# What Now My Love

(French Title: "Et Maintenant"))

English Lyric by Carl Sigman
French Lyric by Perre Leroyer
Music by Gilbert Becaud

Moderate bolero tempo

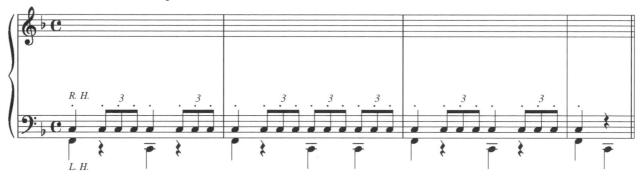

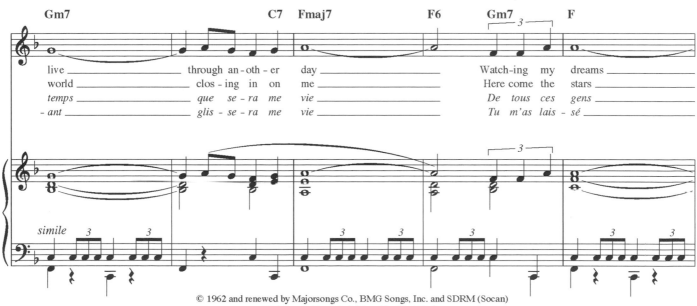

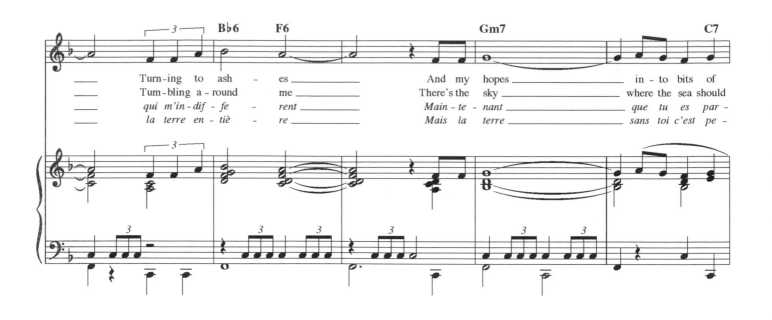

What now my love 2-3

What now my love 3-3

# You'd Better Love Me

*(from the Broadway Musical "High Spirits")*

Lyric and Music by
Hugh Martin and Timothy Gray

# Something Cool

Lyric and Music by
Billy Barnes

Something cool I'd like to or - der something cool _____ It's so

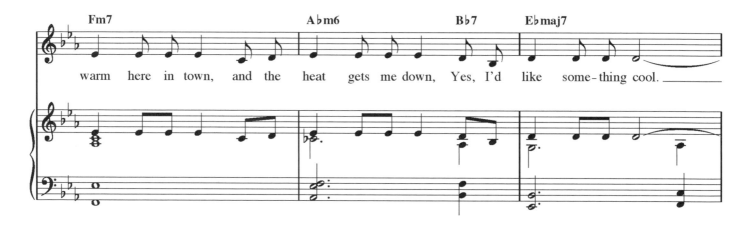

warm here in town, and the heat gets me down, Yes, I'd like some-thing cool. _____

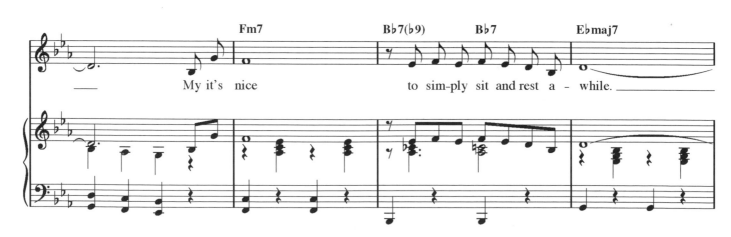

_____ My it's nice to sim-ply sit and rest a - while. _____

Something cool 2-6

Something cool 3-6

Something cool 4-6

beg and beg to take me to a ball    I'll
bet you could - n't pic - ture me the time I went to Par - is in the
fall. _____ And who would think the man I loved was
quite so handsome, quite so tall. _____ Well, it's through

Something cool 6-6

# The Masquerade Is Over

Lyric by Herb Magidson
Music by Allie Wrubel

Moderately slow

My blue ho-ri-zon is turn-ing gray ___ And my dreams are

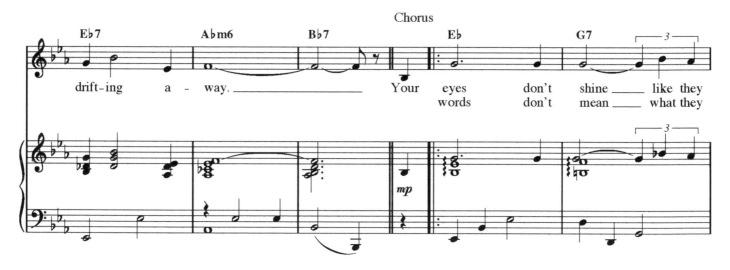

drift-ing a - way. ___ Your eyes don't shine ___ like they
words don't mean ___ what they

used to shine. And the thrill is gone ___ when your lips meet
need to mean. They were once in - spired, ___ now they're just rou-

The masquerade is over 3-3